No Budget Film Making

by

Tom Kennerly

ISBN-13: 978-1501018435
ISBN-10: 1501018434

DEDICATION

This whole film thing, it's just to kill time.
My true vocation, Curly, is thinking of you.

Also by Tom Kennerly:

Fraternal

The Happy Caterpillars

Model Citizen

Swag

The Two Roomer

CONTENTS

ACKNOWLEDGMENTS

Each of the cast and crew that has contributed to my projects brought a concrete *something* to the table. It's one of the great mysteries of artistic collaboration. Love me, hate me, or just don't care; I needed every single one of you. Thank you.

Intro

Why are the books on 'how to make it' always by some guy who you've never heard of? As I tell my nephews, if you have to tell people that you're famous, you are probably yet to be famous. I don't know if you have 'heard' of me or not. You may want go to imdb.com and confirm that I have, in fact, made and signed distribution deals for feature films.

So, famous or not, I present this book because I believe that there is a small gap out there in the scads of books that are available to you, the independent film maker. I refer to some of these sources at the end of the book. There was no reason for me to duplicate their sound advice in specific technical areas. Which lens to use, lighting how-tos, and editing tricks, are all available to you from film school grads and camera geeks.

What those guys tend NOT to have is a plan. Now, with this astounding tome as your guide, you will be a circus master, pied piper, and show runner; the glue that will turn a gaggle of cast and crew into a finished film. What I hope this book does for you is two fold: you can look at specific problems and plan around them; and two, you can start embracing the idea that you can get over any indie film obstacle if you put your mind to it, not just by throwing cash at it.

A quick point, 'no budget' does not mean zero dollar. My definition of no budget means what you and your co-producers can pull out of your rainy day funds over the course of a year. To some this may be 5K, to others 50K. The point is, you keep a tally of your expenses, but don't get yourself all wrapped up in budgets, budgeting, and the devil's own creation, budgeting software. To be clear, however, my guidance is given to help you to your final cut at closer to 5K than 50K. I hope that makes you feel better.

One

```
FADE IN

EXT. HOLLYWOOD PREMIER - NIGHT

Cameras flash as a line of limos slowly unload
their well dressed cargo.  Emerging from one of
these black stretches, starlet (or star) in tow,
is you.

                    KENNERLY(V.O.)
          Yes, you!

                                        FADE OUT
```

Say it out loud. You want the glory, the recognition, the reward, the big moment. I did. (Still do)

I've stood upon the red carpet, although I had to pay the rental for at least one of them myself, and I can't wait to return to the next premier. They're exciting of their own accord, but they're exciting *times ten* when the project is one that you conceived of on your own, and then breathed into life.

No Budget

You can finish and distribute a feature film without a budget. I've done it. I want you to do it. Just remember, no-budget doesn't mean no cost. It will cost you some money. The Kennerly no-budget philosophy is, *worry about the costs as they occur.*

If you make $40,000 a year, and spend $39,500 of it during the course of the year, do you demand the $40,000 from your employer on January 1? It would be interesting, no doubt. But, no, you take a little money in, and apply it to expenditures as they occur. You can make a film that way. 'Film makers' who sit around tweaking budgets with 'budgeting software' are not film makers. They are budget makers. You're a film maker, if you're making a film.

The purpose of this book is to allow you to inch closer, ever closer, to that goal. Silly, wouldn't you say, that one would let the appearance and of structure of a script, or, the ability to use the correct lingo for a few crucial moments, to get in the way of one's dreams? Silly indeed. But, many, many, would-be film makers float scripts out to cast and crew that are quickly written off as amateur, and therefor passed on. Likewise with the crucial first day on a set, when the cast and crew either knuckle down for a few weeks of hard work, or start to rebel, individually or en mass.

Preparation is the key to many different areas of success. Keep my little guide here within reach, keep your chin out, and you WILL look like you know what you're doing on the set. Finish your first film, and you won't even need the guide.

I can't make you into a leader of men, OR into a creative thinker. But I can pass along some of the experience I have had in a way that will make you look as if you have a few more notches on your gun than you truly have. It's no more complicated than that.

Why now?

If you're a camera or computer geek you may want to skip this little section, which outlines my reasoning for abandoning the budgeted approach to independent film making. Basically, it revolves around technology.

Yes, my young film maker, there was a time when you could not shoot a no-budget feature. Really. Did you know that the film stock alone necessary for a feature film shot on 35mm format comes to more than $20,000? Incredible. Then you had to rent an editing bay ($ for rental) on which someone rolled actual processed film ($ for processing) back and forth, and chopped it into your rough cut. Then *that* had to be made into a negative.($)

We now live in the wondrous age of data cards and hard drives, making the barriers to entry into feature film making, well, low enough. DSLR cameras put images onto data cards, and these are uploaded to plain old desktops with software upon which the editing is performed. (admittedly, desktops with huge memory capacity)

Why now? number two: Distribution has REALLY changed. Let's go down to the video store and – whoops – there are no more video stores at *all* in my town. We watch movies on computers and phones even! Cable has 1000 channels! The need for video on demand has not only increased the alternatives for product, but, made self distribution a reality. More on that later.

Writer/Directors: Stronger Then Ever

Looking at film credits is very instructive. I'm that weirdo who is left sitting by himself watching the credits roll, while, you're standing in line tying to get out because you REALLY have to go to the bathroom. One of the primary things you will note is that for some time now, most of the films that score well at the box office have the director credited also as writer. If not, the director will probably be credited as producer. When you see a person who has these multiple credits, you probably have identified the 'showrunner'. This guy is the first person who said, 'what if?', and the project grew from there. I hope you're paying attention right now, because, no-budget film making demands that you be nothing less than a showrunner.

The production cycle of film from concept to premier is longer than you would think. (Of course, if you put my plan into action, you'll soon find out) A great way, perhaps the only way, to ensure that the vision of the writer is carried through to the finished product, is for the writer himself to lay that vision out to the cast and crew. That's what I do. So , let's look at the production life cycle of a feature film at ANY budget level.

Two

The Five Phases

Here we go! The five phases of feature film production are:

Development

Pre-Production

The Shoot

Post Production

Distribution

If you're a planner, your mind should be starting to whirl. Yes, it is true: If you master each of these five chunks one at a time, you will have a finished film!

Here is a list of common tasks in their appropriate phases:

Development

Completed Script

Treatment

Loglines

Rating (anticipated)

Key hires

Lead actors

Pre-production

Locations

Auditions

Offers made to actors

Crew interviews

Offers made to crew

Equipment inventory

Recording media format decisions

Property(props) identified and acquired

Schedule formed and distributed

Cast and crew contact list created

Disposables identified and collected

Catering and craft service planned

Callsheets formatted

Shot sheet finalized

The Shoot

Get the Footage!

Post Production

The mechanical

Visual pickups

Audio pickups

Score and musical cues

Titles

Other effects

Distribution

Copyright Chain

Stills

Posters

Thumbnails

Trailer

Premier

Screeners

If it were only that easy. As you review this list, identify things that you had not considered, or perhaps, are not sure exactly what they be, and find them later in the book. If you are going to complete a film and distribute it, every single thing in this list is coming at you, sooner or later. Your eventual list will probably be three times this size, but this is sure enough to start, so let's get started.

Development

Development is the indie film maker's friend because it is pretty much free. This is the planning stage. If you have your script, start with that, and answer the age old questions; who, where, when, and why. ('what' is the script) Now, this amazing little book is worth ten times what you paid for it, if you only give the next question the most serious of considerations, which is the longer version of why:

What do you want to do with your film?

I see you. I can see you right now. There is a big uhhhh forming behind your teeth. Very common. Let me guess at a few inklings crossing your mind regarding the possible future of your film:

1. I want people to see it,

2. Film Festivals, I guess,

3. Find distribution – whatever that is…

4. OK, I'll say it, fame and fortune!

I've been there, so I apologize for the sarcasm. However, *you need to decide what you want to do with your film*. It really, really, will affect the type of film that you make and how you make it.

I can assume that you ultimately want to commercially distribute your film, because from that, well, will spring the aforementioned fame and fortune, but you may have just assumed that all feature length films are eventually commercially distributed. Not true at all. *Most feature length films do not achieve a commercial distribution deal*. Period. The majority of films that *show at Sundance* do not achieve a commercial distribution deal. Now that's scary.

So, what would one do with a feature length film that is finished?

1) You could have a blast entering it into film festivals that want your type of film. You could get into larger festivals that are attended by industry folks, get noticed, and be asked to pitch them your next idea or script.

2) You could show it at local independent theaters, with whom you would pay a flat fee and then sell tickets to your friends, relatives, fans, etc. This is called 'four-walling' in the industry. You can

even invite local press, but you know that there won't be anyone there from the 'studios' because you would have to have invited them, and you don't know them, or you wouldn't be reading my book.

3) You could self distribute via the web. Via your social media pages, direct peeps to sites that would allow for streaming or other similar type of download. If this is reasonably successful, you could stamp a few hundred DVDs so that your cast, crew, relatives, or any one else (like the author) who is a bit old school can enjoy your art. A low risk, low investment alternative, for sure.

4) Follow my little plan and look for a distribution partner. There will be little or no upfront money, you will probably have to throw your own premiere, and you will wait for months (at least) until you see it available for sale, but this is just about the only way that you have a shot at international distribution or national cable distribution. This was my goal, as the rest of this rambling diatribe suggests. This is the step toward the big time. Film Festivals are just another form of self marketing. Four walling is another form of self marketing. If you're not a self marketer, if you like film making and not P.T. Barnum tactics, then you definitely want a distribution partner.

A note on Producer's Reps. If you have been doing research, the true producer's rep is not as prevalent as he or she once was. Anyone who is not a distributor who says that he wants the exclusive right to market your film needs to REALLY explain to you why he should be given that exclusive right. That explanation should include past successes. It just doesn't make sense that he could pull this off and not consider himself to be either a distributor or a producer. Be cautious. Some folks love the film industry and enjoy matchmaking at this level for a few bucks here and there, but the snakes that have hung around the industry requires that one look very carefully at any one who says that they are a middleman without a brick and mortar office. If you make a feature film, a snake or two WILL find you. Trust me on that one...

A quick comment that I just can't let go; What you want to do with your film can also be asked in this way: *Who are you?* A writer? A director who hates to write? A writer who hates to produce? A tech freak who doesn't mind others in the glory positions? Know yourself before you start. You'll be much happier.

What is a film?

These paragraphs may seem like philosophical rhetoric, but they are VERY important to the no budget mentality. For instance, we no longer use film! It should really just be called a movie, and you a movie-maker. That's one big reason to shake the conventions of the past.

Another is, as discussed elsewhere in this book, if you are really going to distribute a 'film', then you must define it by the list of items – the deliverables – that your distributor requests of you. Waivers, contracts, chain of title, music clearances; It is a monumental task that most 'film makers' leave as an afterthought, as these things are not fun. But without them you can only show the film in your own basement. (legally) And these not fun 'things' are as much work as making a whole other film, trust me.

How about public relations and advertising? Surely, you've set aside money for websites, posters, and the premier? I'm kidding. Of course you haven't. Okay, we'll go the easy route, and submit it to a film festival, and they'll promote it. Really? Have you ever attended a film festival? It's the same price as a weekend getaway, plus the submission fee, plus the fee to attend...

I'm not trying to depress you. I hope that you have said 'that's me' as you read about PR, or traveling to festivals. In a bizarre twist of fate, I have found my place in the world as the duke of deliverables. That is how I define the questions above. In my mind, the deliverables ARE the film.

Three

The Story

Commonly, you will be given advice along the lines of, 'you must have a 'great script'. I don't believe in great scripts. I don't believe in screenwriting seminars, competitions, or 'doctors'.

I believe in story. You DO have to have a great story.

Screenwriting competitions are for those who don't have the desire or skills to turn their stories into movies. The great Tim Burton has been quoted as saying that he 'wouldn't know a great script if it bit him in the – (name for rear end goes here)'. For the writer/director, the script is a blueprint with which your cast, crew, and producers align to your vision. Some painful guidance on your script:

- ⋏ A limited number of Characters;

- ⋏ A limited number of locations;

- ⋏ Probably 'ten little Indians'.

Readers, you will be making one type of film, and one type only, if you want to follow my formula, and that is the format referred to as **Ten Little Indians**.

Ten Little Indians: A group of some sort, gets to a destination of some sort, and makes a wrong turn of some sort, that has them get picked off by a nemesis of some sort, until one of them makes a stand of some sort.

It's been done a thousand times.

It has sold billions of dollars of tickets, rentals, and consumables.

If you want to fight the system, sell this book at a yard sale and go weep over your next script under a swinging light bulb. See you at the car wash. I'll be driving. (that Porsche's comin', I'm tellin' ya)

If you want to make and market a movie, shelve your pet project, and have a BLAST writing 100 pages of bloody fun. It's less of a burden. Deep down you know that at some point you've been entertained by something in this genre, and others will be too. Even my family feature 'The Happy Caterpillars' is a ten little Indians script with the blood removed. Really.

Also:

- ⋏ You can't afford to build sets;

- ⋏ You can't afford stunts;

- ⋏ You can't afford car or traffic scenes;

- ⋏ You can't afford more than a few locations.

But;

- ⅄ You *can* afford fake blood;

- ⅄ You *can* afford sound effects. (appendix)

Limited characters and limited locations is easier than you think. Start ruling out night club and crowded train station scenes, wedding receptions, etc. You will find that eliminating characters helps eliminate locations, and vice-versa. One of my features is actually titled 'The Two Roomer'. Ninety percent of it was shot in one condo which was redressed as a second condo mid shoot. I walk the walk.

This book includes a script writing primer. Enough of the basics are included to allow you to start cranking. The best way to tighten your script writing style is to read other scripts, no doubt about it. A great way to have some fun and learn is to buy a script from one of your favorite films. Amazon has a ton of them. Don't invest in an original, or some collector's version, just a reprint is fine. Also, if you're loving writing you can purchase a more detailed book on writing screenplays; there are many. This book is meant to get your film made, not turn you into a film school graduate. There are enough of those, heaven knows.

Hot tip: Put the odds in your favor, and make sure that your film is PG-13. First of all, PG-13 films outsell R films at a rate of more than 3 to 1. Also, if you do get a television or standard cable deal, it will have to be PG. You can still swear a little bit, and have implied nudity. That's all you need.

Treatments: I hate writing treatments! But, I have to, and so do you. At this level, a treatment should be between a half and a full page summary, that tells the basics of the story. There are some people who will need to know what they're getting into without reading the full script. Treatments are used for other reasons in the big leagues, so its good practice for you. Your distributor will probably ask your for one before you're signed. Speaking of which, you need a...

Logline: I also hate writing loglines. Here's an example: *Three friends are resolving strained relationships during a holiday, when a flash flood strands them, forcing them to truly trust one another.* Loglines came from a time when they were written in a log at the studios, so that producers could keep track of what was pitched to them. You need them in your PR tool kit, and, don't forget, treatments and loglines are FREE. Put them to use.

What if you can't or don't want to write a script?

You're still in luck. The only group of artists more unemployed than actors are screenwriters. You should be able to get the rights to a script for almost nothing, or by giving some points, especially in the Ten Little Indians genre. However, don't forget the parameters above. You may have to agree in advance with the writer to change the script to make it affordable to shoot. Additionally, you will definitely have to analyze and say no to some scripts.

Have a script polished and ready to shoot? Nice. Other knuckleheads are out there looking for funding. Not you. You're a film maker. *You have no budget to worry about.* So you get to move onto...pre-production.

Four

Pre

Pre-production. The very sound of this compound word makes my head, and other parts of my body, hurt. You see, at the studio level, what makes the dividing line between development and pre (as pre-production will be called from her on out) so specific is that little phrase 'greenlight'. That means that money has changed hands. Probably while nursing a hangover (from the greenlight celebration), writers, directors, and producers start making offers to cast and crew and arranging for locations. You, no budget film maker, will be doing the same thing, without the $. Hence the headache.

This is the make or break chapter of this book. As I allude to in other areas of this little masterpiece, there are already all kinds of technical how-to books on writing, budgeting, and process when it comes to film. Unfortunately, most of them tell you how to spend money. This chapter is focused on how *not* to spend money. Your interpretation of this chapter is what will allow you to make a movie without financing. In essence, you must become a pied piper. Let's talk about who you will be recruiting.

Who - Casting

Guess what art form has about as many folks sitting on the sidelines waiting for a break besides writing screenplays and directing? Yes, acting! What does that mean to you? It means that you have one crucial element of your film available to you for almost nothing! Hear my words! 90% (plus) unemployment for actors is a constant, even if those actors live in sight of the studios, right there in tinsel town. At this level of film making, if someone comes to you and explains why you need to suck it up and pony up $ for 'talent', put them on another project, and by that I mean someone else' project. They don't understand how to get it done. There is no downside to hiring talented unknowns. They:

➢ are hungry

➢ are trained (they have the time)

➢ are appreciative

➢ are available

Now, you need to audition them, and look at their resumes, and make sure they fit, and be a pro about working out the details, but man, oh man, is it a buyer's market.

Where are they? I gotta be straight with you; trained, hungry actors with the right mindset are mostly in LA. My biggest hurdle, in Central Pennsylvania, was casting, not funding. So I went to the internet. A fantastic site for actors and film makers is www.nowcasting.com. I won't go into the details of how it works here, but you can manage your submissions, narrow down your selections, and view the actor's reels right at the site. If you're in LA, or close, you just set up auditions and further narrow down your players. If you're way far away like me, you find what you can locally, and then cast long distance. Did I mention – for producers it's free! Every actor should now have a clip available on line for you to view. You may want to make a cheapie trip to LA and meet your finalists, or you can go goofy, like me, cast them long distance, and meet them for the first time in person 24 hours before you shoot. (not recommended) I have used other sites that were really good – they are mentioned in the appendix, but I mention Now Casting here because it is the yardstick for indie producers, in my opinion.

Casting Calls

It is possible in *any geography* to use social media to post a time and date, and have a good old fashioned casting call. Hotel meeting rooms are cheaper than you might guess – my last rental was $50 for four hours. Also, they have tables and chairs and so forth and will arrange them per your request.

Needed:

- ⚔ A camera on a tripod;

- ⚔ A sign in sheet;

- ⚔ Sides (short pieces of the script with which the actors will audition;

- ⚔ An assistant.

So you put your casting call out there, and accumulate the number of people coming, just to make sure you don't end up with 2 or 1000; either could happen. My most recent example yielded just over fifty actors in middle of nowhere Pennsylvania. We finished with five minutes to go for our time slot. Reality: We only found two people we could use. I've had as many as a hundred and only used two. Some of the artists are nice people who are talented, but just don't fit the roles. Some are terrible. Some are nutty. But you need talent.

Hot Tip: Ask for referrals for crew members right at the sign in. Make a sheet like a pre-interview that asks for basic contact info, the actors online pictures or reels, and include this referral area. Actors don't refer other actors, but they can't lose a job to a crew member...

The camera, the sign in sheet, and the assistant will help people feel that you are professional and that they are not being lured to their death. If you have a decent turn out, you WILL need that assistant.

Please don't bet your film on people you are dating. When I say bet, I mean, key roles have to be handled by people who can do it. Just like in any other business, things happen, and it take one HELL of a professional to separate business from pleasure when no one is getting paid. Same goes for friends/favors. I had a twenty year veteran of the stage choke on me the first time he heard me yell action under the lights. A very tough conversation followed. We want to work with people we know and trust – but we can't cast them in a role based on that alone.

Sorry for the diversion. Here comes the numero uno rule for being an indie film pied piper. Please, don't be afraid to offer good, struggling actors:

Copy, Credit, and Meals

CCM is well known in LA by cast and crew. Definition:

- A copy of the finished film, which the cast or crew member can use for his or her own promotion;

- Their appropriate listing in the film credits, (and hopefully on imdb), and;

⅄ finally they need to be fed!

Budgets are tight in – well- everywhere, so feed them during those twelve days, and these cast and crew will feel much better about doing a freebie. The other reason to have snacks and meals and coffee and water on site is that if ONE person decides that they have to run for food or coffee in the middle of the day, mob rule ensues, and everybody scatters. You will lose too much precious time.

You Will Learn This Hard Lesson

We artists – are strange. All in our own way, that's what makes it fun. Except, when artists are strange in a way that screws up your production. This strangeness **will** occur, and it probably will occur on everyone of your productions. Don't tell your cast this, but you REALLY need them. When you're paying people, it's tough to find a rush replacement, let alone when you are NOT paying people.

The tip I am about to give you is worth a hundred times what you paid for this happy little book if you will put it to use. (yes, I'm going to keep saying that) You **will** make an exception, and you **will** get burned. Here is is:

Set the time for your casting call at a time that will be typical for the shoot. If you will be shooting Saturdays and Sundays for a few consecutive weekends, make the call for nine am on Saturday or three pm Sunday afternoon. If you will be shooting days during the week, make it for those days. Whoever shows, gets in. Who ever calls, emails, texts with an excuse, IS OUT. EVERY SINGLE TIME I HAVE MADE AN EXCEPTION TO THIS, I HAVE BEEN BURNED. Sorry. Let me calm down for a second. There is sound logic to this rule. If they can't take an hour or two out of their busy schedules to get the part, really, how will they carve twelve hour days from their schedule to meet the demands of the shoot? I mean, if this were a 'business' job interview, and they couldn't find the time to get on the interview schedule, would they be hired? No. You've been warned.

On to happier casting thoughts. Scheduling aside, one should really treat their cast with all the pomp and circumstance that can be afforded. Here are some ways to do so:

- Ask for them to fill out a PR sheet, including a bio, and other stats that the media would ask for,

- Do your best to afford a very low budgeted, but some sort of meet and greet before the production,

- When an actor is wrapped (done shooting for the rest of the picture) announce this on the set, and have the cast and crew applaud for them.

I encourage you to think of other ways to make them feel like stars. They're not doing this to make you famous, Producer, they're doing this because THEY want to be famous. Remember that, and you will do well.

Extras

Gee whiz, try not to pick (or write) a script that requires lots of extras. If you only need a few, make your crew do it. Maybe you can trade a few favors for these 'walk on rolls'. Make your producers do it. If you do need, say, twenty extras, you better find sixty. Only one in three of those who claim that they are excited about it will show. I don't know why. This is one of those things that you would think would be easy, but for some reason has been a thorn in my side.

Five

Some More Pre

Keys

I make clear early and often that I am not a camera person or an editor. I have to hire these key positions, and I believe that *not* saying 'I'll just do it' has been the reason that I've finished any feature that I've started. No one person can do it all. You must find some key crew. The list at the end of this chapter notes them in descending order of 'gotta have'.

Who - The Crew

Crew are plentiful, but not so eager to work for CCM as actors. Here is how to get good crew to work for copy ,credit, and meals. Most crew are looking to trade up. Experienced wardrobe staff would like to be costume designers. Experienced camera operators probably would like credit as DPs. So find good folks and credit them at the next level. Example: You have a really good guy who holds the boom for you every day of the shoot. Credit him as 'sound supervisor'. (if you don't already have a sound supervisor) Not sure what I'm talking about? There are brief definitions at the end of the chapter.

By the way, if the names of these crew members are not familiar to you, and you have never been on any kind of a set, you may need a 'cookbook'. A cookbook is a book on how to make a film WITH a budget. Scads of those have already been written. See the appendix.

My recommendation with hiring crew is to delegate. Hire your DP, and offer them a day rate between fifty and a hundred dollars. (start low!) This is an important position, with heavy lifting involved. and by signing a contract with (*just a little*) remuneration, they are less likely to fade/quit/ get mysteriously ill. Now that the DP is getting paid, you can ask him to hire his peeps for copy, credit, meals. Maybe a floor to sleep on. These guys run in packs, and you'll usually be pleasantly surprised at the results. On a smaller set, the Director (you) and the DP run the set, so make sure that this is person is on your wavelength.

The DP

The Director of Photography, or cinematographer, is going to define whether or not your movie 'looks like a movie'. For real. This is a tough job at the no budget level. In the big leagues, there are multiple assistants, and a guy whose job it is JUST to push the dolly. (the dolly grip, check it out) on your set, the DP is probably going to do the job of DP, first camera, second camera, and be your light crew. The reason that they are available in the modern era, however, is that lots of dudes and dudettes outfitted themselves with nice DSLR kits, and they would like to put them to use. Have them submit a clip to you for consideration, something that they have shot, not just 'worked on'. The DP is sometimes cranky in the fact that he is working for much less than he should be, so, we must take advantageous of this fact without being ridiculous. I've been lucky. All my DP choices have pulled long days and been hardworkers, and I paid them back because I have something that you too, will have to barter with, which is an imdb credit as DP on a feature. This is THE bargaining chip. Don't forget it. It's what they want. Don't forget this either; you need to deliver.

UPM

My unit production manager, sometimes called a line producer, has been the same guy for the last three films. I don't know that you will have it so easy. The UPM runs the set so that you can film. He gets waivers signed, he deals with locations, he runs for, or gets someone to run for batteries. He is a producer, literally. Finding someone who wants to be a producer will be a golden moment in your career progression, as most people don't even know exactly what it is that a producer does. Probably the best person for this job at this level is your understudy, someone who wants to get in the game, but doesn't have enough particular experience at anything.

Disposables

Your project is going to use paper towels, toilet paper, batteries, trash bags, and five different kinds of tape to the Nth degree. If you don't have a UPM with some experience with this, here's my suggestion, and I'm not kidding. Ask a mom with three kids how she packs for vacation. Also, keep your eye out for bulk deals on this stuff.

A First

First Assistant Director can also be a real stepping stone for the right person who is not a DP or an actor but wants to be involved in your film, and wants to write and direct their own stuff someday. They can be either a girl/guy Friday, or a true leader, but if you are directing, there will be MANY times when you will need this person to run interference, deflect, or just help with the age old, 'how do I do two things at once'.

If you successfully hire a DP, a first, and an editor, you can delegate the rest of the hires to them, and start making a movie.

What - Equipment

The DP and the editor that will allow you to finish a film at this level will be using their own equipment. This is, frankly, the big reason for sucking it up and paying them. They have their equipment for a reason. They like it, and know how to use it.

WARNING: Most DPs are equipment junkies. They will start thinking of 'must haves' that they want you to rent before they even see the locations. Keywords for you to memorize. They alone (again) are worth the price of this book. Start saying them into the mirror with a big smile on your face.

"Not in the the budget."

Digital Intermediate

I'm fascinated with digital intermediate. It still is used at the studio level, I don't know about the high indie level. Here is the digital intermediate process: The production company shoots on film; the film is turned into digital files, just like those put on a card by a digital camera; the files are uploaded to the digital editing suite; the finished film is cut, then rendered digitally, and then *turned back into a film negative.* This is done becaaauuussseee, modern computer based editing machines have many more capabilities with CGI, etc. Also, it's cheaper. So, why shoot on film? Supposedly - uh, well, I don't know. Tradition?

Anyway, sarcasm aside, indie film maker, you're a step ahead. You will be editing in digital because you will be shooting digital. The studios are imitating you!

The only downside to the festering cornucopia of alternatives out there is that equipment geeks get themselves caught up in what to shoot on. *Do not be a slave to technology. Make it work for you!* If your background is in video technology for some reason, or you already have a strong camera body, and want to surf the net for lenses, adapters, and so forth, knock yourself out. I don't enjoy this kind of thing, so, I take the safe and easy way and make my DP my first hire, as mentioned earlier. Nowadays, any director of photography or cinematographer either has his own camera, knows five guys with rigs who will loan them for favors, or has an 'in' to a ridiculously cheap rental. Certainly you should have some serious meetings regarding why he is recommending his specific choices, as well as check out examples of that particular equipment combination's footage by the artist, but please let this expert contribute where his knowledge exceeds yours.

I have to tell this story to give you an example of how this equipment is already out there waiting for you. One of my 'day' jobs between films not so long ago was as a bartender. (of course!) My dishwasher was one heck of a nice guy, who we'll call Sven. Sven had no car. His girlfriend dropped him off and picked him up from work. Sven had no money. He carried his girlfriend's credit card around with him, for emergencies. These emergencies usually resulted in a pizza run. I talked to Sven here and there, and soon found out that he *owned an SLR a full notch above the camera I was using on my next shoot.* Do NOT sweat the equipment. It's 'out there'.

From here, the choice of camera, a review of the script by the DP, and a review of your confirmed locations will dictate the lighting package. Again, beg and borrow if possible. I spend money for lights because I shoot long days for a SHORT period of time, and therefore my daily rental doesn't add up to that much. Note: The new DSLRs are a great alternative for shooting low light - their capabilities exceed those of six figure cameras in this area. Also, almost anything else might be low budget, but nothing I can think of rivals the quality and flexibility of slr/dslr.

Editors

I pick my editors as early as possible. A lot of folks like to 'worry about that later', and for your first project, I would say that you might have enough on your plate, that getting images onto the card as close to your script as possible should be the priority. I've done it that way. But there are advantages to your editor meeting with your crew if there are effects (green screen), specific tones or themes, and other more complicated things going on. Also, you may find a good editor who doesn't want to even hear that much about your project until it's shot, as so many indies never come to fruition, and he doesn't feel like getting jerked.

Anyway, just like with a DP, you will only be hiring an editor who has his own rig. Why? Anyone who can edit at this point in the industry has how own rig. They may ask for a couple add-ons that they need to process your specific project. This is the other person that you are paying, so depending on the fee you negotiate, it could be you or the editor that eats this. Buy 'this' I mean a ninety-nine dollar software add-on, or some memory, not an eight core processor.

Sound

Bonus! Sound has changed in favor of the indie film maker. Digital is a huge leap forward from analog. (for the purposes of our discussion, Analog means 'tape', and digital means ones and zeros)

ANY digital sound storage is cheaper, more flexible, and will give you better sound than previous magnetic tape based recording systems. If you're lucky enough to find a sound guy who has done film, you will probably find him through a referral from your editor or DP. If not, you will need to cobble together a rig, which is much simpler than it once was. This rig will contain: A directional microphone, a boom pole and cabling for the recording device to be out of the shot, and, the recording device. That's it.

Zoom makes a variety of hand held digital recording devices that are popular on the set, but one can also turn a laptop into a very inexpensive recording device with inexpensive software and a simple interface. Microphones are probably the component that I would try to borrow here, as the level mike you want for your movie is probably about $600. Put your crew on the case. If you can't finagle one or rent one cheap, a $200 mike got me through two features, and I'll bet one of your crew already has one, so don't sweat it. Booms are cheap or can be made. Make the investment of padding and gloves for your boom man, however. Cable slaps, rubs, and other bumps will sound like stampeding buffalo when you get into the editing bay. Take it from the guy who knows.

Also, you will want to record in stereo. I mean, your phone probably records in stereo, so the cost is not a concern, but you, your sound, and post team want to discuss this so that there are consistencies for post. At this level, I really recommend that you resist the temptation of surround, although it is financially feasible. It's one complication that you don't need on your first feature.

Hot tip! One great way to fish for this equipment AND be a good citizen is to let local bands submit original songs for your soundtrack. Due to the digital revolution that we previously discussed, half of every band out there has their own gear. You may also find some good stuff for your film. *Soundtrack* to be discussed later.

Negotiables

Producer Credit

Veterans of Indie Film will not be as excited about this, but you never know. You have at least a dozen varieties of producer credits to bargain with (see appendix), so why not use them all? In my experience this has been enough to gain a commitment two out of three times.

Points

Look at you, big-shot producer, negotiating back end. The phrase back end was generated by the fact that the movie has to 'make money' before the points can be divvied up. There are 100 profit points in a movie that is marketable. What if you offered your DP $500 cash, five points, and an associate producer title? Sure sounds like a better offer than plain old $500, doesn't it? At a higher level, you will also be giving incentive to all of those with points to get the project all the way to distribution, if they ever want to see any of those five points turn into dollars. You will need your contract resource book to do this the correct way via a producer agreement. Of course, just like in the big leagues, cast can be lured with points, too.

Reciprocity

The best negotiable in the world is one that also works in real life: You scratch my back, I'll scratch yours. I'm bringing this up because it can sometimes be hard to get behind someone else' project when one (or more) of yours is languishing on a back burner. No pay. Long days. I understand. Suck it up.

Reciprocity can only help your film career! Worried about this possible project not fitting your high standards, or not being what you want to be 'known for'? No one knows you anyway, knucklehead! When two alpha artists meet, why not take turns being second banana for each other? Be script supervisor on my film, and I'll grip on yours. Everybody gets to go to the set. Twice! Twice the experience, twice the networking with other new cast and crew. Besides...

...*No one can predict the success, or lack of success, that will come from a film project.* Famous examples:

Francis Ford Coppola (then relatively unknown) was DYING to make a film called 'The Conversation'. The only deal he could cut was to make one for the studio from a best selling novel, and only then would the studio fund 'The Conversation'. Coppola said okay. The film he 'had' to make? 'The Godfather'. He *did* make 'The Conversation'. Both are great movies. Which do you consider more 'successful'?

Steven Spielberg, after initially being excited about the project, was also reluctant to work on turning a certain best seller into a 'movie'. He told the studio that he wanted to makes 'films', not 'movies'. David Brown, then Universal Pictures executive famously told him, 'If you make this 'movie', you'll be able to make any 'film' that you want. David Brown was right. 'Jaws' became the highest grossing picture ever (at that time) Fun fact: Spielberg wanted to drop 'Jaws' for the project 'Lucky Lady'. Wow. Fun fact number two: The term 'Blockbuster' was first used to describe the runaway success of 'Jaws'. How would we live without it?

Summary: At this point in your career, lend your shoulder to any project which you possibly can, and encourage your 'circle' to do the same. You never know...

Where

Locations can be another friend to the film maker, if they are outside of Southern California. Look, folks, to be in this game, you have to be a salesperson in some way shape or form. Presented correctly, you can have homeowners, and other property owners, wishing for you to include them in your project and shoot on their property.

Presented the wrong way, letting someone shoot on one's property sounds like a giant pain in the butt, which, *it is.*

Take your time with locations, there is no studio clock ticking. Film is a visual medium, and you really have a chance to be creative at this level. Scouting for locations is another almost free endeavor that the indie film maker should really sink himself into. Visit during different times of the day for lighting purposes, record background sound, picture your crew setting up and working there. (electricity available? What kind of noise will ruin shots? Etc.)

Look into local permits. Film makers love to brag about how they didn't pull permits, and got away with it, but why not first see how much a permit costs, if anything? Being sent home will cost more than a permit, I assure you.

As far as personal residences and businesses go, LA home owners are a bit jaded, and may expect an exorbitant day rate. In any other area of the country you will more than likely get away with bartering for an extra role, or mention in the credits. Be creative.

Warning: this may sound humorous, but it is true; *you will not be invited back to film!* They may be polite, or they may be pissed, but you will have problems calling in two weeks to re-shoot, if you miss something. Make no mistake, film crews are mini traveling circuses. Please, give yourself enough time to shoot everything in a particular location the first time around, or you'll be blowing your budget fixing every nick and scrape (real or imagined) in your borrowed location.

The Script Supervisor

You can shoot without one, but if you can find one, things will be so much better. The odds of you finding an experienced script supervisor and getting them into two weeks of twelve hours days for almost nothing, are low. Much more likely is that you will discuss with your DP and editor as to the makeup and nature of the reporting you will be using. Examples of these reports are easily found on online, and then you bend them to your personalities. Maybe you can trade someone a bit part in exchange for these duties. Maybe the DP wants to bring someone along. But this little misunderstood position will keep you from realizing two weeks after you have wrapped that you skipped a whole page, or that your lead started a scene in a red shirt and ended it in a blue shirt. (this is continuity) If you need to know more about what a script supervisor does, make that your homework. All that I can do is strongly suggest that you promote someone who has some common sense into this position.

Continuity

Everyone becomes a continuity expert the second day on the set. Unfortunately, 'I think she was wearing...' doesn't cut it for continuity. I shoot out of order (as will you) so I need to keep wardrobe continuity in check, in particular. Other continuity items are day/night, prop food and drink, curtains open/closed, beard shadow, and of course hair. Luckily, digital photography has become our friend. Use a digital camera or a phone if you have to, and take a photo EVERY TIME someone is ready for a shot. Upload it to a tablet or laptop, and name it by scene or character number. Two days later, someone TRYING to be helpful, will say, 'I think she was wearing...'. So the scripty goes to the picture files, and you pull the evidence, and shut the big yapper of little miss helper. Or, you're wrong, at which time, you grit your teeth and say thank you. Either way, you avoid a text from your editor in sixty days which contains the word 'problem'. By the way, given a choice between someone filling out daily shot reports and someone taking wardrobe and set stills, I choose the stills. Hint.

Stills

Still photographs are essential to the eventual PR and distribution deliverable needs of your film. My first feature found my distributor disappointed with my stills. My guy focused too much on behind the scenes. *You will need stills of the characters in character during shooting.* Any trained DP will know that this small invasion of his territory is necessary. Book two or three still photographers if necessary. You can't go back and take stills once you wrap! Again finding someone with skill AND time to do it will be tough, but you can't go back and shoot stills once you wrap! You don't need stills from every shoot day. The trick to doing this the no-budget way is to just ask the still photographer in on two very different looking shoot days, in fact, make them half days. That should easily give you a couple hundred or so stills to pick from. What's that you say, can't the DP just use the SLR to shoot stills? Not gonna happen. You will be running behind every minute of every day for the whole shoot. Think I'm kidding? You wait.

Food

Get your credit card out. You need the equivalent of craft service, which is water, coffee, and snacks for the cast and crew *all day*. You will feed them at the meal break, something that could be lunch or dinner, and you may shoot long enough to have to bring in the semblance of a second meal toward the end of the longer days. Don't forget, you promised copy, credit, and *meals*. This is still much cheaper than a salary, and nobody has to leave the set for a break. Very important for shooting the number of pages you need to get through on that day.

Holding

Holding is a big break room. It can be inside or outside, weather permitting. It is where the cast and crew that are not required on set can hang out, keep their stuff, eat, etc. It should be in the proximity of bathrooms, as well as water, coffee, snacks. The further the break room is from your set, the less your first A.D. will be screaming QUIET. The closer it is to the set, the faster you will get your cast to the set. Frankly, holding is dependent on the locations you choose, just don't forget that you will need this area one way or the other.

Crew List

Here is the list of crew that you will need in approximate order of importance, starting with the most important. Without the first five, I really wouldn't recommend starting a shoot. Their set nicknames are in italics.

Director – You?

Director of Photography (Cinematographer) – *DP*

Unit Production Manager - *UPM*

Makeup Artist – *MUA*

Script Supervisor - *scripty*

Production Assistant 1 – *PA*

First Assistant Director – *The First*

Craft Service/Catering – *Crafty*

Wardrobe - *Wardrobe*

Camera Operator – *First Camera*

Property Master - *Props*

Production Assistant 2 – *PA*

I've previously mentioned that if you didn't pick up this book already having some idea of how a set operates, that you may need a cookbook. I hope that you also see that if you know enough to hire the right keys, they can recruit and hire the others, and you can concentrate on higher level stuff. Delegate when you can, for the sake of your movie and your sanity.

Six

Shooting

The shoot itself may be the easiest part of the five steps involved in bringing a feature to fruition. There are several reasons for this. Probably the most important is, that's where the energy is. Cast and crew, digging deep to create something. Barely second to that is that cast, crew, and you, have been doing all kinds of boring dirty work, like auditioning, and answering ads, and reading contracts; and you're all finally here, on the set! Your and your team will find the time flying by, and endure hours that you would never consider enduring on a j-o-b. You'll find all the things that make your shoot effective were really addressed by me in pre, and I hope that they were therefor addressed by you in pre. We need to talk a little about scheduling, however.

Scheduling

The thing is, you're a beggar, indie film maker. And beggars need to cater somewhat to the schedules of those who are pitching in. Also, indie film maker, you can't afford the lighting necessary to shoot day for night, or night for day. Also, you may take one tried and true approach, and just shoot weekends for a month. So mirroring the big leagues with ironclad schedules, and scheduling software is not just a waste of time, it won't work. But we need to organize, right? Right.

I implore you to take this task on yourself, and here is why. One of the drawbacks to no-budget film making is that if someone screws up, no shows, or is a total retard, firing them is not that much of a punishment. You could literally lose a whole day of filming if *one key person* does not show up, and you can't afford that.

Phone lists

Start a spreadsheet the day after you decide to start making a film which contains the phone number and email for every one involved. You will thank me for this.

Call Sheets

Essentially you will need to put together a call sheet for every day that you are filming. What you want on your call sheet is your choice, I 've included a sample of mine at the end of the book. You should print a copy for all of your keys, everyday. It will save you asking and answering a thousand pages. If you review the who, what, where. when, and why that we have just been discussing, you will simply be laying that out on a sheet of paper. Now, you look at them and arrange them so that your people who have day jobs, your people who are coming in from out of town, and your location agreements line up in the correct way. You will very quickly understand why it is a rarity that zero OR multi-million dollar projects shoot in order.

The way that you will stay on schedule is via page count. Your script is 105 pages. You can shoot 7 pages a day. You have 15 shoot days. Schedule one extra for back up. You have a 16 day shoot. Need to get it done in 12 days? Looks like you need to hit 9 pages a day. I believe 7 page days are do-able. I believe planning for 10 or more is not realistic. Your call, sheet, which is really just a plan for the shoot day, will reflect this.

The following three recommendations will solve a lot of your scheduling problems. Two are copied from 'the big leagues', one I stole from a behind the scenes documentary. Hey, that's what they're for, right?

One: The following will, in my opinion, multiply your chances of finishing your project with a smile on your face by a factor of – I don't know – at least pi. So here it is. You will structure your shoot days the way that sit-coms have taped for years. For the first half of the day the actors will rehearse while the crew sets up around them. When you get the scene down, and the actors blocked, you break for lunch or dinner. The cast then gets made up and the remainder of the day is the shoot. If you have more than one set for the day you will have to adjust accordingly, as well as make time adjustments for your day/night needs. Bonus, *if you shoot like this, you will be able to hire folks who cannot get away from a day job.* They will not be there for rehearsal, but can probably be there for the whole shoot.

Example: My make up person was fantastic, but she could not get time off from her day job. Using the above schedule, she rocketed over to the set at approximately five, the cast finished dinner right about then, and we shot until midnight. By the way, I hope you will let your freshman participants know that a 'day' on the set is twelve hours. At least.

This style of shooting also means no time-consuming table reads, rehearsal days, or rented rehearsal space. Yes I am a genius, thank you.

Two: Bring everyone who is available, everyday that they are available. Cast and crew. They'll come. There's a movie being shot! An actress can hold the slate. The boom man can be an extra. An extra can run for lunch. Bring them; the most wonderful problem you can ever have is that too many people show. Don't have them hire sitters or miss work to be in holding, but bring them if they're available. You will thank me for this.

Three: Index cards. I love 'em. Each of your scenes will become an index card, with the characters in the scene, script page number, length of the scene in pages, and description upon it, for starters. You then, usually with your DP, sort through these and assign them to days. The indie world shoots seven to ten pages per day. So, you keep from wasting time, or over booking yourself, by laying your cards (literally!) on the table, and seeing how the shoot day plays out. As scenes are completed, they make their way off of the table. Keep them with you in a rubber band. It will make you look like an organizational genius. It will also help you complete your film. It will also help you with an ugly situation that is probably going to occur which is...

Shooting without a slate or a script supervisor. A slate is commonly known as 'the clapper'. It has the scene and take # written upon it – we've all seen one. The odds, at your production level, of you having someone available for your entire shoot, to clap that thing, with the appropriate scene and take number written upon it, is next to impossible. You will try to get the scripty to jump out of her chair and do it, and then things will move too fast, and you DON'T want to lose your scripty, so you just stop slating. Guess what? It's okay. The digital revolution has changed things so that post is possible without slating. There are countless web based articles about file organization, that address the modern world of video based shooting, which editors have adapted into their work flows. These methods haven't replaced script supervision and slating, but made it just possible for post to occur without it. I'm just telling you, I haven't always had the manpower on a feature to have both a scripty and a slater everyday. I hope you do, but keep those index cards ready.

Stills

Again, stills require discipline. If you have a dedicated art department or wardrobe person, they can take the digital stills of wardrobe and sets at the beginning of each scene for continuity. In the modern era, these are thrown on a laptop and referred to as needed. This is cheap insurance. You *will* find yourself having to finish, re-shoot, or match a scene two weeks after you first shot, and EVERYONE will guess wrong if you guess at who was wearing what, and whether a candle was lit or not. NOTE: *Don't waste your time with behind the scenes photos.* It's amateur. It takes time. People may care what Oscar winners do between takes, they don't care (yet) what you or I do. IF you get a distribution deal you will be asked for action stills, not behind the scenes stills. I warned you.

And yes, I'm an Ax Grinder. Hey, it's my book.

Legal

I don't give legal advice and I am not an attorney. My umbrella comment is, you are setting upon a business venture that will eventually encounter all of the same contractual, tax, and risk elements of like businesses.

Additionally, there are creative elements that surround the 'life' of something that has been created by a group of people. To this end, within your grasp is one Mark Litwak, who has produced a number of guides geared to indie film, the essential being 'Contracts For the Film and Television Industry'. You will NOT GET A DEAL WITH A DISTRIBUTOR WITHOUT GETTING MANY OF THESE CONTRACTS IN PLACE. You will not get a real DP or professional actor on set without these contracts. Summary: CYA with these contracts. It is a royal pain, but do it, and you will have walked the extra mile that those who have footage languishing in storage *did not.*

Pointer: Make 'em sign before they can walk on set. Cast and crew alike. Just bring a laptop and thirty dollar printer to the set. (just use your stills laptop)

Seven

Post

Alrighty. You're wrapped. The twelve hour days are over, you're mad at a good thirty percent of the people who walked onto the set, and you're eating ramen noodles. Take an hour off, you deserve it.

Okay, break's over. It's time for post. 'What?' you say, 'The editor has the footage, What do I need to do?' Well, in the big leagues, they have a title called 'post production supervisor'. Ninety percent of what this person does is crack the whip. You will soon find out why they hire this person. You will hear more 'I can'ts' and 'I don't know's' and 'we have a problem's' than you ever dreamed. A lot of this can be prevented by properly setting expectations, just like in real life. Here's what we need to accomplish in post:

A mechanical: This is the movie put together in the correct order, with a quickly decided sequence of angles, to make sure it's 'all there'. Essentially, to find out what you missed. Oops, we don't have a master shot of the house exterior. Uhoh, we should have shown the radio, we can't tell why there's music in the scene. We don't have a clear shot of Jenny cheering at the basketball game. So, now we schedule a day of...

Pickups: Probably just you and the DP get in a car, and go through a punch list of little pieces that were skipped, came out poorly, or had a nasty shadow or mic boom in them. 'Wait a minute', you say, 'we're going to recreate the basketball game, just so Jenny can cheer?' No, you're not. Jenny lives three states away, and there were fifty extras. So you, the writer, and the editor, are going to write around this. I assure you, they do it at the ten million dollar level, so don't feel bad. You'll be amazed at how unnecessary the cheering shot can be.

Score and other music: I have been a lucky dude when it comes to music. I have found musicians who badly needed scoring credits, and signed them for nothing or almost nothing. I have one fantastic song from one fantastic group in my first feature that is correctly signed and released. IT IS HARD TO DO. For good or for bad, there is a TON of free and almost free music to be downloaded from the web that is digitally mastered. I mean a whole library can cost as little as twenty bucks. My recommendation is, try to give a local band or composer a chance, but if they look like they are moving slow, or they show a reluctance to sign the rights away, let it go. Also, I have to tell you that many composers will want to wait until you have picture lock, or everything completely timed out before they start. Can't do it. You need to get them a script, and get them to visit the set, so that they can start the ideas flowing. If not, say bye-bye. Obviously, their score can't be correctly matched until your last picture cut is available, but in the best of all worlds, it should be ready to be 'laid in'.

I hope this sounds like a complicated process to you, because it is. You must think about this when choosing an editor. How is the workflow going to work between him and the composer? The three of you should meet before the shoot if possible and definitely at the beginning of post. One more warning, your distributor will look for signed releases on all of your music.

Titles: You can't afford anything other than the simple titles that your editors program can generate for free, so there's nothing to worry about. At this level, the more straightforward the titles are, the more professional you look. Bonus: When you had your cast and crew sign their waivers, they filled in a line as to how their name should appear in the credits. You sill be reviewing all of these, because YOU will be sending a document to the editor from which he will create the opening and closing credits. This is your last chance to give someone a producer credit or something else they may have earned along the way. Don't forget the 'thank yous'...

Other effects: My last film had some fading and other visual things that had to be specially reviewed by me with the editor. You may be in a situation where an artist who is not the editor contributes something visually, like a graphic artist. Make sure there is a delivery workflow set up. These artists do not reach out to each other until they are told to do so, I assure you.

Rough cut one: There are many different ways for you to look over rough cuts in the digital world, but if you have more than three rough cuts, then you chose the wrong editor, or he chose the wrong project. I've watched it with the editor and given notes, and I've watched it on my own, and reviewed the notes over the phone. The only 'rule' here is to let the editor know that there will be at least two roughs, and anyone with common sense will understand why.

Rough cut two: What I need to pop into your brain now so that you can pop it into others is this: You still need to sell this, and to say that the editor will never have to open the file again after he delivers it to you is never going to work. Something is probably going to be adjusted. It could be as simple as the company who buys it wanting their logo in the film. FYI, the time to shake hands and part ways with your post team has not yet come.

The Screener: The screener is your best rough cut with sound. It is color corrected, has titles, and you will knock out a couple dozen screeners on DVD.

Eight

Distribution

Distribution has changed A LOT. Speaking of 'a lot', 'On The Lot' is an old school phrase that is a little dream of mine that just may never happen. It involves me driving through the gates of the studio in my restored sports car, with the security guard tipping his cap to me with admiration, as I glide over to the reserved parking space in front of my bungalow. A studio deal.

I may as well pine for a studio contract with RKO.

So, if you are thinking that sometime, not too long after you screen the final cut, you will be haggling over advance checks with lots of zeros in them, in a bidding war with distributors who are salivating to acquire the rights to your quality no-real-names-production, well, let me be gentle.

You're out of your mind.

So, in most cases, you will be deciding between a mid level distribution company, and self distribution.

Good News!

There has been no better time in history where you can look like you have a distribution deal, without getting a distribution deal, than right now. BUT: The dream remains. Your name on the big screen; the Ferrari, (Porsche?) the adulation. It may happen, but for this film (again, if this wasn't your first serious film, you wouldn't be reading this) and for your sanity, plan on the lowest level of distribution. IF you strike gold, great. But, once again, *plan* on the lowest level of distribution. Self distribution. It's not so bad! And it can easily be profitable.

Now, even though you're planning on self distribution, there is no reason to hide your light under a bushel basket. How does one do that? Dig. Here are a few strategies. Pick the one that is 'you':

The Guide: Before you shoot, get the download or the paper version of a distributor's guide. No excuses, Amazon has it. It's not cheap. That's why you buy it *before* you shoot. You won't have the money afterward. Also, while you're waiting for your editor to finish, you will go through the guide and find those listings that cater to your genre and accept screener submissions.

Next, you email them a link to your trailer, asking if they would like to see a screener. They will respond if they do, with a submission form or disclosure. *Then* you send the screener. Sending screeners blind is too expensive. Then you wait. Then you wait some more. Start polishing your next script.

Warning: The first thing that film makers try to do when they get into the game is break in. The second thing they do is set up some kind of a scam to get money out of other film makers. It's crazy. Script contests are almost all put together by frustrated film makers to make a couple of bucks on your lofty dreams. So it is with those who want to sell you contact information. The information changes quickly, and there are so many electronic sources coming and going, that no one can give you a 100% accurate list. I can tell you that as of this printing, The Hollywood Reporter(tm) has a Distributor's Guide 2010 available. There may be others out there, but they're the only one that I can recommend, and they've been doing it for many years. They don't make one every year. It was by using their 2004 guide that I got my first distribution deal. These guys are not fly by night, there info is the real deal, or at least it was when they went to press.

Research: You should be watching films in your genre for LOTS of reasons, but the biggest payoff will be if you take notes of all of the companies named in the beginning titles. 'A Blind Bull production'. 'In partnership with Dot Matrix Films'. These are clues to distributors who found distribution for that film. You take this short list and run it through imdb to see if there is a clear cut sales agent. Google the address, and you have a place where the screener should be sent. You know that they take your type of film, because they successfully sold one.

Slowcooking: Also, you can give yourself a page on several online indie film sites. If you list your project on Mandy and stage32, you will get some inquiries. I must warn you that a lot of these inquiries are going to be trying to sell you something, but if you attach a link to your trailer, and your trailer is good, some legitimate distributors will come your way. My recommendation is to set this passive strategy while working other more direct strategies. Don't forget, youtube is the second largest search engine in the world. You are really blowing a chance for pass along value if you don't have a quality trailer posted there.

Self Distribution

So, time goes by, and distributors have either not contacted you, or, they've officially passed. How do you know it's time to self distribute? I can't give you a formula. Something in your head will say; I want this product to be available, and I'm tired of sitting by the phone. (By the way, *many* distributors will email you a prompt no) Maybe it's time to do it because you want to move onto the next project. But once you do self distribute, it is much less likely that you will be picked up for traditional distribution. The cat is out of the proverbial bag. So think long and hard before you decide on self distribution. In any case, there are all kinds of folks who will let you sell the DVD or market the download online as of this printing. Amazon is continually adapting to the self published world, including film. Createspace is a clearing house for Amazon that will guide you through the process of uploading for either hardcopy DVD distribution or Video on demand. Createspace is an option. As of this writing Vimeo had just announced their revenue sharing streaming platform. I also like indieflix.com.

What's the difference between self distribution and getting a distributor? It's a heck of a question, as technology and distribution alternatives continue to blur these lines. I would say that the difference is, if you sign with a distribution company you will have an ally who wants to put you into a large income bracket, or they don't make money. If you self distribute, the platforms that 'accept' your film will set you onto their site, **and you will still need to do the lion's share of the promotion.** Think about what you will and won't be willing to do at this point.

What I Would Do...

I have some of these recommendations for you because I've been through all of the contortions, disappointments, and sheisters. I encourage you to be bold, we have only one life to live. However, what I would do if I could return to my first film's distribution process, is this: Work the options I have listed above starting with, 'guide', them 'research', then 'self', going to the next step when you feel that it's time. In the end, by letting a company like Indieflix keep their 'cut', all of the responsibility for fulfillment is in their court, and you can start planning your next epic.

How long to wait until you resort to self? Big studio films often wait for a long time for the right distribution window, so prepare to wait. And, to repeat a point I made earlier, only a fraction of all the feature films completed see a legitimate distribution deal.

But try for a distributor first. You never know…MOST IMPORTANT. *Remember, it's your product!* Do with it *what you want*, not what you think you should do.

* The various websites mentioned here are all listed in the appendix.

Deliverables

Unfortunately for deliverables, this list of demonic hurdles comes at the end of the project, when the typical indie film maker is ABD.(all but dead)

PLEASE, think about these deliverables before you hire your first actor, crew member, or intern.

Think about it. When the dust has settled, everyone will have gone on to other projects – maybe even you – and only you will be there to attend to these time consuming and potentially expensive details. The deliverables *are* your movie! Not the script, not the shoot, not the cast or crew.

IMPORTANT: Ask to see the deliverables list before you sign the distribution deal. It may scare you. It should. By the way, they are negotiable, but only if you don't sign first, right? You've been warned.

Here are examples of some deliverables, A significant combination of them will eventually be requested by your distribution partner:

➢ Completed film on digibeta*

➢ Completed trailer on digibeta

➢ Copyright registration for the movie

➢ Copyright registration for the script

➢ Script rights agreement

➢ Composer rights agreement

➢ music cue sheet

➢ synchronization agreement

➢ Time coded dialogue list

➢ Certificate of Origin

➢ Stills

- ➤ Synopsis of Film

- ➤ Quality Control report from lab

- ➤ Poster and DVD cover art

What's that you say? What's a digibeta tape? Guess what? There are half a dozen digibeta formats. What's a synchronization agreement.? What's a music cue sheet look like? Haven't bothered to copyright the script yet? Did you know that it will take (at this writing) up to 8 months for you to get the hardcopy?

Good news. The cookbooks have all this information in them. 'Contracts for the Film and Television Industry', as previously mentioned, is a must have if you reach this stage of the game. Plug the phrases above into a search engine, and start thinking about them now. What is and isn't important on the set becomes much clearer when you know what form all your hard work will be taking.

*Admittedly, digibeta is being required less and less. It's for developing countries whose platforms have not upgraded to true digital. I leave it in as a possibility because indie film makers sometimes have projects with ONLY foreign sales.

Nine

PR

Public relations. If you get into pre and your team is excited, the following conversation will come:

'I saw (insert name of crappy movie) and IT got onto (insert name of mid level cable channel) Why can't our project do the same?'

I'll tell you why. Nobody knows about you, or your team, OR your film. That nasty little thing that appeared on cable was drummed up, pushed, exploited, talked about, posted, and reposted. You get the picture. Type my name into any search engine. I come up first, and I do not employ any SEO service. I've been yelling about myself for years – you had better think of ways to do the same.

Former producer partners of mine who are great, talented people are no longer partners of mine because they didn't believe in PR. They wanted to 'be on the set', and create. What do you think would happen if they were googled? I know, I've checked. Yeah.

So, if you want to get onto that cable channel, you had better get good at PR, or partner with a loud mouth who is. There's no way around it. For starters, have an account on:

- facebook

- twitter

- any free blog site

- youtube

- mandy

- productionhub

- withoutabox

- imdb

Also, you wouldn't suffer from buying one of those '100 ways to promote yourself' types of books. Don't be the best kept secret in town...

imdb

When I got into the game, I had two seemingly insurmountable goals. One was too get my SAG card, the other was to be on imdb. At the time imdb was an independent third party that cared not for hype, subscriptions, or marketing. You or someone else involved in a project submitted to editors who would review your submission suspiciously through their monacles, and maybe, just maybe, 'let you in' to the club. There you would be, listed in the same historical film bible as James Dean and Cecile B! Equally as important as the ego component was that other indie film makers could search for your credits, and immediately see if you had really 'done anything'. Many meetings hinged (really) upon a preliminary imdb check. Cast and crew alike.

Well, times have changed in several ways:, the two most notable being, Amazon acquired imdb; and I can't believe I'm saying this, but I don't rule people in or out based on imdb status anymore. However, other people do, so you need to get onto imdb. Here's how you can do it as quickly as possible:

1. Finish a film of any length, submit it to an approved film festival on withoutabox*. Upon acceptance, it, along with listed cast and crew, will qualify you for imdb status.

2. Subscribe. Go to imdb.com, and their marketing machine will quickly tell you how you, yes you, can have an imdb page for $/month. Warning: Anyone with my experience (which is not all that much) or more can read through your BS, which will be worse than not having a page at all.

*purchased by imdb, which was previously purchased by Amazon. Get it?

Stills

We indie artists do not do a great job of this, because everyone is busy making a movie. But I will keep harping on the stills subject, because you will eventually need a poster, an online poster or thumbnail, and screener graphics if so desired. One of the hardest things in the world is to find a DIY article for making your own movie poster, but it can be done with software you already own. Working graphic artists outside of the studio area of LA don't make movie posters, so beware. You want your poster to look movie poster like, not to break new ground. If you can't picture it hanging up in a local theater, take another path. The online poster of thumbnail is a stripped down one, in the modern era, those tiny credits at the bottom or top have no chance of being read.

Ten

The Traps

The subtitle of this chapter is 'Sweet Revenge!' Several people playing at film maker caused me a heap of wasted time and energy, early on, trying to enlighten me with their unproven formulas for success. *I'm* the idiot; as I listened, at first. They made a tough venture tougher, as I looked for support and guidance, and instead found these boobs. I hope they read this book and see themselves in the time, money, and energy traps listed here, as they keep thinking that a finished film is somewhere in their futures.

You and I, as independent film makers, need help. It is near impossible to do it all by yourself. So you find some like minded people, who will let you tell them what to do while they are earning nothing. What they want is the glory of their name in the titles, the adrenaline rush of the set, or to pay their dues and gain some experience. Probably they want a combination of all three. So you meet. You agree that a small cadre of you is the producing team. And then, the problems begin. I have listed some of these detours here. There are others.

Now that I have that off of my chest, I'm thrilled to have you learn from my experience, but if you have 'been to film school', I'm warning you, you will be a little uncomfortable. Oh well.

Here they are, in bold:

It would be nice to have a production office

What the heck for? To play film maker? To audition starlets? To have pre-production meetings? With who? Because you are reading this I can deduce that YOU DON'T HAVE ANY MONEY FOR A FILM. Why do you want to spend money? Don't. Instead, do what the 'playahs' do in LA (and Pennsylvania), and meet at a coffee shop with wifi. There are many producers who started legitimate careers with nothing but a cell phone and a P.O.Box. By the way, a P.O.Box is not a bad investment whatsoever. If you get a deal, you will need an address of record at which to legally receive communication AND royalties for seven years. I haven't lived anywhere for seven years straight. Ever. Think about it, itinerant artist.

We should print a business card.

Sure you should. If you want your mom to be proud. Other than that, put the money into production. No one who has heart, and wants to help with your project, wants or expects a business card. This is a minor offense, as you can probably procure 500 business cards for fifteen bucks, but think about the purpose. If you're attending a festival, and hoping to run into potential crew, then great. If you just want to build a paper empire, then get into multi level marketing, and you can REALLY waste your time.

We should have a website.

See above. Do people really build websites anymore? No distributor will demand that you have a website. You need a finished film and a distribution deal, not a website.

You should do a rewrite.

Do a rewrite when someone gives you a check that is inline with WGA standards. (the current minimum for a budget feature length screenplay is $54,000) Otherwise, tell them to go home and play producer with their sister's dolls. Rewrites, in the no budget film world, are something to do while 'you're figuring out financing', which you'll never figure out. Rewrites kill time. Don't get me wrong, you need a great story. If someone asks you for a rewrite, just ask them if they like the story or not. This isn't a screenplay competition.

We need a budget.

Budgets assign funds. You have no funds. You need no budget. Read the above line ten times until it breaks down the brainwashing. There's nothing to budget! There are going to be expenses as you make the movie, and you need to know enough about pre, production, post, and deliverables to know that they are coming. If you think that you are going to deliver a budget feature film without incurring *any* expenses, then you are an idiot, and no budgeting exercise will help you.

So and so is available, but they need (insert dollar amount that you can't afford)

Good for so and so. You don't need them. Heck, *I'm available.* Actors are always facing ridiculously high unemployment, and most crew, particularly those with less than a decade of experience, are facing very high unemployment. Saying 'if we could scrounge up 5K for Miss wonderful', is a *big* trap. Why not scrounge up 50K, if that's the case? Stop wasting time thinking about it, politely move to the person who will do it for free.

There was an old 'name on the box' method of indie film making, in which you would offer a television actor 10K a day to be in your film for 3 to 5 days during his hiatus. (in between episodic TV seasons) The trade off was that the actors made some quick money, and you could market the show with these known names, distributors would be enticed by the two prospective known names on the DVD or VHS 'box'. Don't buy into it!!! I know of several producers, as I write this, who have not found distribution for finished films in the 500 K to 2 mil range, and there are current sit-com stars and best actor Oscar winners 'on the boxes'.(I'm not exaggerating) Besides, you can't afford it anyway. Stop thinking about it. Now.

Don't Cry Wolf

You've finished your script. You love it. Maybe you found the perfect script. Maybe you found the perfect actress. For your own sake, please, **hold** on the Public Relations. Feeling that you may have a project underway becomes exciting and you want to brag about it like a first time pregnancy. Resist, and you will be happier in the long run. Do you really want to announce that you're shooting in the fall, and be standing in front of the DP you were going to use in December, when nothing has happened? Even worse, do you want to drag hopeful actors down to an audition too early in the process (you'll use the excuse that it will create energy and help the project along) only to have them waste half a day, and possible take time off from work, for something that may not happen? Even if you couldn't care less about others, you will soon have a reputation as someone who can't put together a project, and you can't afford that when you're asking for free and almost free help. Don't get ahead of yourself. Do the work, and you won't have to act like you're in charge of something, you really will be in charge of something. Crying Wolf is closely related to…

Let's Just Shoot The Thing

Gotta love a man (or woman) of action. In fact, most of this meandering diatribe is intended to inspire you to 'make a movie'. But: Being on the set does not necessarily a movie make. Be honest with me and I'll be honest with you. It's fun to be on the set! The set is a high energy place where hardworking talented people combine their skills to make magic. Yelling 'that's a wrap' on the last day of shooting is not the end of the road. If you have read the precious chapters, you know this to be true.

Do the work in development and pre-production. Have a post production and distribution plan, that's all I'm asking. Can it change? Sure. But there is much more footage that hasn't seen the light of day than there is in the bargain bin at the X-mart, I assure you. Don't just plan the fun parts, plan the whole project.

Then shoot.

Eleven

Writing Your Script

Okay, people, telling someone 'how to write' is just left of telling someone how they should be human. It's a really broad area that no one person has perfected. The learning is in the writing. BUT, luckily for us, we have chosen feature film as our medium, so that script or screenplay writing is something that we only do to serve the movie project. If you reread the last sentence and acknowledge it, you will be further along than ninety percent of the schlubs dabbing away at their tablets in So-Cal coffee shops. We're going to tell the story with cast and crew, not with script writing software.

The gist of this chapter is going to be that you have an idea that needs to turn into a movie, and the correct way to represent those ideas to the others involved is in the format of a script. The big hurdle, of course, is getting started. Der's more than one way to skin a script. Here are a few that I have used:

Outline it: This version is for you, if you have an idea of how the plot will go, but don't have a strong feel for the characters, dialogue, and other details. Divide a piece of paper into three areas, and start making notes of where events occur in the story in their appropriate act, one, two, or three. Is it all lopsided? Maybe the story is, too. FOLLOW THE RYTHYM of the three act format. Leave it at your peril. Anyway, once you start filling in how to get from that scene in the first act, which you can see in your mind, to that scene in the second act, which you can see in your mind, you will fill in the dialogue, flesh out the characters, and have a script.

The Germ: A germ for our purposes is a scene, or a character, or, even better, a relationship between characters, which you see in your mind's eye. Get this 'scene' down with all of its details and dialogue. Take a breath. As you reread it, you will find that creating the scene forced you to describe locations, other characters, and scenarios that will now open those related scenarios in your mind's eye. This key scene spreads, becoming your script. The one danger with this method is that you are rolling the dice that your beautiful vision will spread to approximately ninety minutes. There are fifty million dollar pictures that suffer from being too long because someone was in denial regarding the story being three-act appropriate. The upside is, I believe this method is the most fun.

The Routine: I have found this method to be ideal for me. Once I know that I'm going to start a script, I do a little math, and decide on X number of script pages per day. Then I stick to that pace as closely as I can. Once I (or you) start to roll, there is a great feeling when you make yourself stand up from the keyboard, and let the mind wander for twenty-four hours, before going at it again. This is particularly satisfying when writing in mystery/thriller/horror genres, where you will have the latitude to choose amongst suspects, killers, victims, etc. It's also a great tool when you have a deadline. Ninety pages divided by thirty days; even I can do that math.

You will find out eventually if you are a writer or not. We do not all excel as writers. We may all have a story to tell, but it doesn't mean that we are good at getting it onto paper. This is the time to find out if you should be the scriptwriter on ANY project. But, please, give it a try!

Writing partners. I don't believe in them at this level. I'm not saying it's never worked, and I'm not saying it isn't used in the big leagues, I'm asking, what's the purpose? There's a saying in the business world that committees squash good ideas and bad ideas alike, and that's why I don't believe writing by committee works for the purpose of an indie film. If you think someone is better suited than you for the project, then just let them write it.

Twelve

Formatting Your Script

FADE IN

           TOM
I am REALLY going out on a limb here.
All kinds of folks who know what
they're talking about, as well
as folks who THINK they know what
they're talking about, will object
to me just quickly giving you the
basics for scriptwriting.

           YOU
Really? Why?

           TOM
Well, people from all areas of the
industry get hung up on looking
for, waiting for, and crafting the
perfect script. However, weeping
over, picking at, and rewriting
scripts doesn't get movies made.
I will repeat my attitude. At this
level of film making (no budget) I
believe in great stories, not great
scripts.

```
                    YOU
          So why should I worry about
          correct script form at all?

                    TOM
          Excellent question.  It almost
          sounds scripted.

SFX            Laugh track.

                    TOM(cnt'd)
          Well, seriously, the answer is, you
          need a cogent, properly formatted
          script to attract cast and crew.
          This is a 'selling' script.  Then,
          you will make a few changes, such
          as adding scene numbers, and turn
          it into your shooting script.
```

Okay, I started this chapter in the script format just to show you
that there's no 'magic', everything can be scripted. On the next
page is a basic scene. My comments will be in this font, which is
Times New Roman. My script - as well as yours - will be in this
font, Courier New, 12 point. Courier Final
Draft is also acceptable. NOTHING ELSE!

FADE IN

INT. JIM'S KITCHEN – DAY *(scene heading, or slug line)*

Sheena whips the coffee pot against the far
wall, where it explodes with a CRASH and
TINKLE of glass. *(this is he action)*

                    JIM *(character name)*
          That's real mature. *(dialogue)*

Sheena storms out of the kitchen and slams
the bedroom door on Jim. She screams at the
top ofher lungs, as Jim simply shakes his
head. *(action)*

                    SHEENA (O.S.) *(means Off Screen)*
          I hate you!

                                        FADE

The short scene that you read above is 95% of what you will need
to know for the typical script. Really, that's it. The basics occur
over and over again. If you are using word, the various tab stops
are at five character stops in the increments which you see. Note
that you will be typing into and printing to standard size 8.5" X
11" paper. If you use Final Draft, it will set them for you
automatically. Whether you want to invest in a script writing
program is completely up to you. I used plain old MS Word for a
decade. Let's learn a few more basics.

Voice Over (V.O.) and Off Screen (O.S.) are going to appear in almost every screenplay out there, so let's get them down. Like above:

> SHEENA (O.S.)
> I hate you!

Sheena is off screen, or out of the frame – in the bedroom - but can be heard. Voice over is a little different. An example of voice over:

INT. JIM'S BEDROOM – DAY

Sheena is sobbing into her pillow.

> JIM (V.O.)
> I walked down to the
> drugstore for more smokes,
> and let her cry it out. Dames.

V.O. is for some one commentating from the past, the future, or another 'place', not simply off screen, basically.

Alright, another common tool that is not used enough, in my opinion, is 'stepping on'. Stepping on will add some much needed realism to your dialogue. People don't always talk in the neat little sit-com ways that are represented on screen, so one way to make dialogue more realistic is with the use of this comment.

INT. JIM'S KITCHEN - NIGHT

Sheena and Jim look at their hands as they
sit across from each other at the kitchen
table.

                    SHEENA
        I'm sorry, Jim, I shouldn't have...

                    JIM
              (stepping on)
        No, no, it was my fault.

Very Important! Give your first speaker enough dialogue to BE
stepped on. Only giving Sheena the line 'I'm sorry...' doesn't give
Jim much to step on, does it?

One more common, and important device is insert, particularly in
the modern era of computer screens

and cellphone faces being, well, inserted into films. So:

Sheena and Jim stretch their hands across
the table, and both smile as they hold each
others hands tightly.

INSERT - Jim's cellphone VIBRATES on the
kitchen table.

BACK TO SCENE

                    SHEENA
          Oh boy, I know who that is.

If you're insert is the end of a scene, you can leave out 'back to
scene', and simply start the next slug line.

Okay, one more basic. Sound effects can be noted with the simple
capitalization of the required sound within the action.

Sheena is on her bed, dabbing her eyes with a
tissue. She hears the apartment door
CREAKING open and SLAMMING shut. Sheena
closes her eyes, and reaches for her phone.

A quick comment. The first time that a character appears, their
name is in all caps. This should be followed by a brief description
for the reader. VERY IMPORTANT FOR A SELLING SCRIPT,
RIGHT? You want your reader to picture this in his or her mind's
eye. Once you're on the set, no one has to picture it, the damn
actor is right there. Are you starting to see what I mean by selling
and shooting script?

The apartment door opens in slowly. SHEENA,
25,end of the day tired, leans against the
door until the latch CLICKS, and sighs.

This is more than enough to get you started. You'll learn more
along the way.

Wrap That Rascal

Note: Tablets have REALLY changed the way we are reading scripts, there's no doubt about it. It costs money to print scripts! Don't do it if you don't have to. I would politely ask your cast and crew if they want a hard copy script. They will probably decline. So, why am I including these instructions? If you get lucky and a professional of any sort says that they will consider your project, you will probably be asked to deliver the hardcopy. It's only done a certain way...

The wrapper of this package is literally your cover page. VIP #1, DO NOT try to flower this thing up! No color, no large print, no logos, no graphics. Nada. Also, use only white paper. If you feel that you need to ACTUALLY make a cover, use white card stock. Only white. Anything else says amateur. So, what's included? The title, in all caps, then 'by', then your name. These items are centered. At the bottom of the page, right justified, is your contact info. Your name yes, again, address, phone, and email. That's it. Really.

Okay, VIP #2 comin' at you right away. A do-able script is about 100-120 pages. No one will even look at anything over 130, and you really don't want to be under 90. A page is about a minute of screen time, roughly, so 120 is a full two hours, and a movie that is two hours plus is a LONG movie. Time for my soapbox. There are trained screenwriters out there scrapping for a chance to get their scripts into the hands of executives that they work right down the hall from. THEY are conforming to the three act, less than 120 page rule. If you are not, you have an even worse chance then they do, right? Think about it.

Okay, stay with me now. Part of your conforming package is the application of some #4A brads. They're harder to find than you might think! (unless you live in Hollywood or Studio City) With a plain old three hole punch you will make the appropriate holes, and insert and flatten the tangs on these brads. Do I need to get on my soapbox again? I didn't think so. By the way, when you bind your first script with these brads, you will understand the reason for the wide left margins which all professional scripts have.

I'm going to get a little philosophical on you. As I alluded to earlier, scripts that are actually made into movies go through a progression. They start as 'selling scripts', which are used to raise interest, then go through revisions, then eventually will become 'shooting scripts'.

Now, which kind of script do you think we should be working on at this point? You are correct, the selling script, because, as I mentioned in episode one, you will be 'selling' your cast and crew on working on your no or low budget set, even if you are not trying to actually sell the script to a studio. DON'T let someone who thinks they know about 'the game' talk you into inserting scene numbers, camera angles, and the like at this point. VIP #3: That is - wait for it - amateurish. Directors and cinematographers determine shots and angles. Not writers. Describe what is happening in your movie in the action, not with 'HELICOPTER SHOT'.

Now that I've given you this lecture, I want to remind you that you probably will NOT be putting brads in your scripts until it's time to shoot. In the modern world, we pass scripts around via email. If, however, you get a shot at submitting to a higher level of pit viper, you'll be prepared. Equally as important, you'll be prepared for your shoot, where printed copies are, of course, needed.

Thirteen

Directing

Personally, I was very lucky with respect to learning the ropes on the set. Thousands, and I am not exaggerating, of 'film school' students have had to beg and plead to just get a PA job or non paying intern job for a glimpse of a studio level set. As an extra, I was sent their five times a week for about two years, and at times, given direction by some of the most experienced in the industry. (I was also jerked around by some real jerks. I'll tell all in another book) My point is, I'm not making up the contents of this chapter.. The following is how it's done in the game.

How do I know this works? It was not so long ago that I gathered a cast and crew for my first feature film, including a tiny bit of funding. At noon on the first day, we were ready. Everyone looked at me with 'well?' in their eyes. I copied the things that I'd heard directors bark when I was an extra, and low and behold, it worked. Copy me; you'll be fine.

So, you're ready to shoot your first scene, day one. You will review the following with your DP so there are no surprises. Let's construct the first sequence, all building up to, you guessed it, action.

Ready on the set

This is a preliminary call. It simultaneously means, quiet, settle in, stop your adjustments, and 'tell me now if something's wrong. Can also be set, or setting, for short.

Sound

This call is necessary if you are not just using 'camera sound'. Meaning you have a separate sound recording device that will later be synched. Your sound man will reply with 'Sound speeding' or 'sound set' I prefer speeding, it means that sound is rolling.

Camera

You are checking or telling your camera operator to start recording or continue if he already is. He will respond with the infamous, 'rolling!'

Background

This cues everything that is NOT your speaking principles for this scene to start their movement. This list includes extras, vehicles, props, set sound, anything that should be in motion BEFORE the first word of the first line of the scene. This is your chance, director, to make sure that you don't blow a good take.

Action!

Alright! You're about to 'get one'. Important: if you're on a budget set, and dealing with cast and crew with little or no experience, you will have blown takes by people who don't wait for action.

Especially at the beginning of the day/scene/shoot. The tip is, I stretch the last two calls into one long sentence, Background aaannnndddd, Action.

Background...and...Action

Your talent will not start until you stop speaking, hopefully, and you won't blow a take. (or embarrass the excited actor or actress) Nice! You got a great take. Of course, you need to yell 'cut', right? WAIT!

This is more technique than a basic, but I'm throwing it in for free. At the moment that you are satisfied that the scene has reached its conclusion, wait for two beats. In 'the game', it's not a 'second' it's a 'beat'. Why do we wait? Primarily, editing. Your editor is linking all of the components of your masterpiece together, remember? He will need some overlap or 'tail'. Remember how we called background and then action? This gave us some 'lead' for the same purpose. So, we have now waited a beat or two and cut. Ok, say it.

CUT (or CUTTING)

There you go. Go get some coffee. Wait a minute, don't forget, you're the director, every one is looking at you for DIRECTION. Several things could happen here, and I'm going to list them pretty quickly, so come back to them as you need to.

Going again

   or

Back to One

or

Resetting

These simply mean another take of the same scene from the same angle.

Turning around

This means, same scene, DIFFERENT angle, probably the reverse.

Moving on

Can be interpreted in different ways, but I use it to say that we have finished that scene but the same specific location is being used.

New set up

This means that the crew ARE moving. It could be thirty feet, it could be thirty miles, but they need to re-set camera, lights, etc.

Picking up

Sometimes it is not necessary to go all the way back to 'from the top' which, as you can tell, I don't use. You will instruct your cast and crew how far back to go.

Picking up from 'you heathen,' and, continuing action!

This is a cue for the post crew that they aren't 'missing something' when they find only part of the scene, if you have a script supervisor, they will note that this is a 'pick up' NOT a new take.

Continue the roll

Continue the roll is an alternative to cut. It allows you to briefly cue or adjust the cast, without causing a new take, or asking the crew to stop/start. Only used for a very brief instruction.

Example: "Continue the roll, Annabeth, a little more volume please, and continuing – action!"

That's a Wrap

This is said at the end of every shoot day, as well as at the end of the whole shoot. Also, when an actor is done for the day, you can let them know that they 'are wrapped'.

Fourteen

The Most Important Chapter

I saved this chapter for the end, because I know what you DON'T want. You don't want another 'Go get 'em, tiger' book, or chapter even.

Well, too bad. Because, little engine that could, you NEED to get active. By choosing to make an indie you are definitely embarking on a journey of a thousand miles. Like a grade point average, it's okay if you pull a C in some areas, as long as you pull an A in others. Of course, you'll be recruiting for those in which you are completely untrained. (in my case, holding and/or pointing a camera)

Getting back to why this chapter is the most important: You need to manage yourself. Making a film, to repeat myself, is nothing but project management. Where most fall down is that the list of to-dos is very long, and we tend to lean toward the things we like to do. We stay busy, but none of the other stuff gets done. And there's tons of other stuff. So, what we film makers need is a routine.

All-stars in many, many walks of life, will gladly tell you that they have a routine, and give up the details, but most interviewers are more interested in who that all-star is dating. I'm not dating right now, so let's talk about my routine.

Every day of my life I get up, squeeze a baseball hat onto my melon, and go get coffee. That part is not hard, I love coffee. I usually inhale a bagel, and then I write down three things that need to get done that day that will advance one of my projects. That's it. Then I jot down other things that are more content related. That tiny routine, of thinking about what needs to get done next, simultaneously prioritizes, reminds, and gives me a chance to consider how I can work these items into my lifestyle. (translation: day job) They may be small items, they may be big items, they may be part of a really big item, but they are quantifiable and achievable.

Example:

1. Edit pages 20-30 of 'The Devil wears Flip-flops"

2. Update producer's agreement for Dave Davison.

3. Email updated producer's agreement to Dave Davison.

Yes, *I know you can do that.* So do it. EVERY DAY. That's 3 times 7, or twenty-one things you will accomplish THIS WEEK towards finishing your film

Okay, I know you *said* that you can do that. Why haven't you? You didn't need me to write this book to inform you that you want to be a film maker. You already knew that. I repeat, why didn't you do twenty little things last week that would move your film forward? You need a routine. Yes, it takes conditioning. But get started, and you will thrive on it.

That's a wrap

Much more important than picking up this book for a few pointers, will be for you to put it down and start working on your project. I humbly submit that despite my opinions on the things that will help you along, however you finish your film and get it into distribution will be 'the right way'. Literally, whatever works. When it does work, I hope that you will, in turn, pass on those things that have worked for you. See you on the set.

Sample Call Sheet:

How Blue, The Moon

Callsheet

Producer - Chris Doerner

Director - Tom Kennerly

Crew Call: 8 am

Cast Call: 9 am

Report to: Kennerly's Condo

Set	Scenes	D/N
Felicia's apartment	12, 14-17	D
Felicia's parking lot	13-18, 19	D

Cast	Part Of
Storm Philips	Chili Peppers
Thelma Realuns	Felicia McGruber
Scott Hankins	Burt

Extras/Special

Special effects MUA - Cindy Crawfish

Glossary

Abbey Singer – The next to the last shot on a shoot day. Abbey Singer was a crew member who consistently called out 'martini', the actual last shot, prior to the actual last shot. Hey, she's better known on Hollywood sets than other crew members, and almost all actors...

AD – Assistant Director.

Background – As a noun, a professional term for extras. Also a command, as shots involving extras will have 'background' called before 'action'.

Block – In theater or on the set, blocking is the paths which the characters will take through the set. 'Hitting one's mark' is following the blocking the way it was rehearsed. Crucial for the camera to see what you want it to see.

Bounce Board – A silver coated, lightweight board used to reflect light onto a specific portion of a shot. Bounce boards are used at all budget levels, but are a particular must have for the indie film maker.

Callsheet – A daily sheet, copied for all producers and crew, to summarize the who, where, and when of the day's activities.

C47 – A term meant to haze newbies and give light entertainment to crew members on long days, a c-47 is simply code for an everyday household clothespin. You read it here.

CCM – Short for copy, credit, meals.

Copy, Credit, Meals – The way in which no and low budget film makers frequently compensate cast and crew for their time and services. Copy is short for copy of the film, credit is the fact that you will be credited in the films titles or end credits, and meals, of course, that you will be fed something, probably high carb, while on set.

Costume Party – A period piece in which a considerable amount of the budget goes into wardrobe and other related art department spending.

Craft Service – Smart film makers at every level keep the cast and crew working by having water, coffee, other beverages, and snack items available on set at all times. The first time somebody leaves the set to run for coffee, and three others put in an order, and then two others go along for the ride, will be the last time you shoot without craft service. The name is derived from this service being a requirement of the various 'craft' guilds and unions on union projects.

Crafty – short for Craft Service.

DP – the Director of Photography, or cinematographer. This is the guy who really studied, light, motion, color, and perspective, and lends his artistic expertise as such.

Development – Of the five stages which comprise film production at any level, development is the first.

Digital Intermediate – In order for the powerful and multi-featured digital editing software programs to be used on true film footage, this footage must be turned into digital files for editing to occur. A print (or negative) may then be struck by converting the digital cut back into film, or analog state. Hence the intermediary digital stage, or, digital intermediate.

EP – Executive Producer. The money man!

First – usually '*The* First'. The first assistant director. On medium to large sets, the director will be behind his monitor scratching his chin, while the first is out pushing and barking.

Five and Dimed – not heard much these days, but a favorite of the author's. Process in which someone reads the first five and Last ten (dime) pages of the script, so that if asked, they can converse as if having read the whole thing. (Don't five and dime me on this one, Horst.)

Grip – Grips support the camera department and the lighting department by overcoming the location's mechanical difficulties -

dollies, booms, other rigging - so that the camera department can focus on smooth shots, and lighting can get their cans exactly where they are needed. On larger sets, the Key Grip manages the grips.

Holding – Mainly for extras, but a place where anyone who is not involved in filming at that particular time can be held, far enough away so that noise does not affect the shooting, but close enough so that they can be brought in immediately after the First AD screams for them.

Honeywagon – A portable trailer that that holds the self contained bathrooms for location shooting. May also contain the dressing rooms for lower than star level actors/extras.

In – The DP, first camera, or first AD, or any combination of these will look through the camera after the shot is set, and make sure that things that are not supposed to be 'in' the camera's frame are not, and that things that are supposed to be 'in', are in fact 'in'.

Logline – One compound sentence describing the movie.

Martini – The last shot of the filming day.

Mechanical – A mechanical is even 'rougher' than a rough cut, and is the first assembly of what was shot during production following the script from being to end.

Mechanical – A mechanical is the simplest of 'cuts'. The footage is laid end to end and edited together to make sure that the whole movie is 'there'. The roughest of the rough cuts.

MUA – Abbreviation for makeup artist.

Out – Out of frame. Q: "Should I move that plant?" A: "Don't worry, it's out."

OTS – abbreviation for 'over the shoulder', one of the more popular shooting techniques.

P and A – Stands for Prints and Advertising.

Prints and Advertising – Once a film is finished, the minimum cost of going into theatrical distribution was known as the cost of prints and advertising; the cost of the film copies combined with the advertising to support the film can easily rival the cost of the film itself. Note: Digital 'prints' have lowered this cost dramatically.

Pancake – a small box, usually part of a set, used for raising equipment just a bit.

PA – Production Assistant. the PA is the low man on the totem pole on the set, and the variety of things they are ordered to do expand and contract with the needs and complexity of the set.

Post – Post production. Everything that goes into the final cut after principal photography has wrapped.

Pre – Pre-production. After being green lit, the organization of a project so as to get into production.

Producer – The are many types of producers in the game. A definition that I have used that stands up over time is that a producer's job is to acquire all of the resources with which to produce a film or video project.

Screener – A complimentary or promotion copy of a film for the purpose of promotion or review, or gaining distribution.

Script Supervisor – This person sits at a desk like station with a small light onset, and follows the script for the rest of the cast and crew, remaining as true to the shooting script as possible. The script is also usually responsible for the shot reports.

Scripty – Slang for script supervisor.

Sides – Short pieces of a script that are used for auditioning, usually one to four pages.

Slate – Several meanings. 1) The clapper has changed quite a bit over time, but used to be a small chalkboard or slate, now usually a combination of dry erase and digital. 2) during auditions, 'slating' means looking at the camera at the beginning of the audition, and stating your name, character you are reading for, etc. 3) Producers or showrunners consider the projects that they have in the pipeline at any given time to be their 'slate'.

Showrunner – When someone is a combination star and producer of a sitcom or movie, or perhaps writer/director/producer or a movie. Everyone else 'gets in line with' the showrunner.

Stinger – Piece of electrical equipment that allows for the input of several lights.

Theatrical – The Holy Grail. Studios are designed to plan for theatrical distribution, but Indie Film Makers consider this winning the lottery. This means that your film is replicated into multiple prints, and put into a number of theaters at one time. the term would usually apply to this happening domestically.

Treatment – a short description of the script or movie. They may be one paragraph, or as long as ten pages, to fit the purpose of gaining interest in the project.

VOD – Video on demand.

Waiver – There are many types, but if you sign one, you are giving up your rights, or 'waiving' your rights, for example, to future compensation.

Appendix

Recommended Online Resources

www.amazon.com

Need I elaborate?

www.createspace.com

This site will guide you through the process of uploading your film, it's artwork, and other required details for sale on Amazon. Read the split rights deal that you would be agreeing to CAREFULLY. However, I think it's a great low aggravation distribution alternative.

www.imdb.com

Still **the** place to see check references and resumes, and wild claims. It isn't the litmus test that it once was, but still a great resource for indie film makers and, more importantly perhaps, plain old fans of cinema.

www.indieflix.com

A well known aggregator and distributor of Indie Films

<u>www.itunes.com</u>

A distribution alternative, one can also make their film into an itunes app.

<u>www.nowcasting.com</u>

This site is golden for casting. The owners are conscientious and helpful. Even if they weren't, the site works great!

<u>www.marklitwak.com</u> Mark Litwak is a fantastic resource in the not too exciting but extremely necessary area of CYA before, during, and after filming. His book 'Contract for the Film and Television industry should be in your hands NOW.

<u>www.mandy.com</u>

long time indie film site that will let you update the production status of your film for PR and distribution purposes.

www.productionhub.com

Well known site for finding cast and crew, used equipment, and anything else that you may need fo finish a film.

www.somsontech.com

This is the parent company of the Zoom recording device line of products

www.sounddogs.com one example of the sound that is available for your final cut. Amazing selection and variety is out there. Shop for the best package bargains!

www.stage32.com

A nice networking site for you to post your projects and its needs over the course of it's life cycle.

www.vimeo.com

as mentioned earlier, this well known video sharing site will now let you stream your videos and collect royalties for it.

www.withoutabox.com

Withoutabox is a platform for getting film festivals together with film makers. If you are doing the festival thing it is a must have. There are other PR benefits simply by being listed. Join it for free, and navigate. You'll see.

Recommended Reading and Resources

Independent Feature Film Production, by Gregory Goodell, St. Martin's Press

- The most comprehensive production guide I have seen. Use it as a resource! If you try to read if front to back you may burst a blood vessel. It is packed with great, specific, technical information.

Rebel Without a Crew, by Robert Rodriguez. There is no substitute, Rodriguez finished his first feature on a micro budget *before digital*! A gritty inspirational read.

Contracts for the Film and Television Industry, by Mark Litwak. This book is gold. You must have this if you think you're going to get a distribution deal, and you *should* have it before you step on the set. I've used it since day one.

Hollywood Distributor's Directory, by the Hollywood Creative Directory Staff. See if you can get one used, discounted or otherwise cheap, but get the latest version! This information ages quickly...

At this writing all of these were available at Amazon...

FILMOGRAPHY - KENNERLY

Director

Not Love, *feature film*- 2014

The Happy Caterpillars, *feature film* – 2012

The Two Roomer, *feature film* – 2010

Writer

Not Love, *feature film* – 2014

The Happy Caterpillars, *feature film* – 2012

The Two Roomer*, feature film* – 2010

57 Sunny Days, *short* - 2007

Producer

The Happy Caterpillars, *feature film* – 2012

The Two Roomer, *feature film* – 2010

57 Sunny Days, *short* - 2007

Made in the USA
San Bernardino, CA
03 February 2015